SRA OPEN COURT READING

First Reader

Table of Contents

Clouds, Rain, Snow, and Ice 3

A Good Day for Kites 8

Deserts 14

Snow Is Good! 20

Hurricanes 26

Glossary 33

A Division of The McGraw-Hill Companies

Columbus, Ohio

www.sra4kids.com

SRA/McGraw-Hill

*A Division of The **McGraw·Hill** Companies*

Send all inquiries to:
SRA/McGraw-Hill
8787 Orion Place
Columbus, OH 43240-4027

Printed in the United States of America.

ISBN 0-07-602779-1

1 2 3 4 5 6 7 8 9 POH 10 09 08 07 06 05 04

Clouds, Rain, Snow, and Ice

All clouds are made of small drops of water called droplets.

Small wispy clouds hold a little water. They are called cirrus clouds. Big black clouds hold a lot of water. They are called cumulus clouds.

When the droplets of water in the clouds get really big, they break free and fall to the ground. They are raindrops.

This pond is filled with water from the rain.

When it is very cold, the water falls
to the ground as snow or sleet.

When it is very cold, the water in ponds and puddles will freeze. It turns to ice. The water is solid so you can skate on it. Have fun!

A Good Day for Kites

"The leaves are red and yellow," said Ryan. "But it feels more like summer than fall."

8

"Check the thermometer to see what the temperature is," Mya said.
"It is 80° F! That is warm for October," said Ryan.

"It is windy, Ryan. Look at the wind sock. The wind is pushing it out. Today would be a good day to fly our kites," Mya said.

"Let's go get them," said Ryan.

10

"Ready, set, go!" Ryan yelled. "Our kites look like wind socks in the sky!"

"Our kites are going the same way as the wind," said Mya. "They look like the real wind sock!"

"What a good day for kites!" said
Ryan. "The temperature is warm. It is
windy and our kites are flying high!"

Deserts
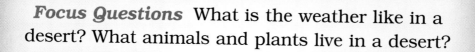

"What is a desert?" asked Miss Cozy.
"The desert is hot," said Joe.
"The desert has lots of sand,"
said Tony.

"You are both right," said Miss Cozy. "The desert can be hot and the desert can have lots of sand."

"Some deserts are cold and rocky Some deserts even have mountains. But all deserts are dry," said Miss Cozy. "Most deserts have less than 10 inches of rain a year."

"Do deserts have plants?" asked Joe.
"The desert has plants," said Miss
Cozy. "Desert plants are good at
storing water. A big cactus holds lots
of water."

"Do deserts have animals?" asked Tony.
"There are lots of animals that live in
the desert. Some live near water holes.
Many desert rodents get their water
from the seeds or stems they eat.
Camels can go weeks without drinking
water. They get their water from green
plants too," said Miss Cozy.

"It must be hard to live in the desert," said Joe.

"Not really," said Miss Cozy. "The plants and animals that make the desert their home do just fine!"

SNOW IS GOOD!

Joan put on her winter coat and ran outside. "The snow is growing deep," she said. "When will it stop?"

"Snow is like rain falling from the clouds," said Mom. "Only snowflakes are frozen drops of water. The snow will stop when the air is dry and the clouds are not so full of water."

"It is cold," Joan said. "Let's make
a snowman before we freeze!"

"Wet snow is good for making
snowmen," said Mom. "Dry fluffy
snow is good for taking a walk or
going for a sled ride. Whee!"

22

"What about all the plants and animals?" asked Joan. "I am afraid they will freeze. When we are cold, we go inside to get warm."

"Snow is good for animals," said Mom.
"It is like a blanket. Groundhogs and
moles sleep under the ground all winter.
A snow blanket keeps the wind and cold
from them. Squirrels have heavy fur
coats. Snow in the trees helps to keep
the wind and cold from their nests."

"Snow is good for plants too," stated
Mom. "A snow blanket keeps the wind
and cold away from plants."

"Are you ready to go inside?"
Mom asked.

"I'm ready for a real blanket!"
shivered Joan.

HURRICANES

A hurricane is a violent storm. It has
swirling winds and heavy rain.

Hurricanes begin in the ocean.
Most hurricanes happen in the late
summer or fall. That is when the
ocean water is very warm.

Hurricanes are very big. During a hurricane, fast winds begin to blow in a huge circle over the ocean. A hurricane's winds may blow 200 miles an hour! Some hurricanes have winds that are even faster.

The middle of the hurricane is called the "eye" of the hurricane. The swirling winds do not go into the eye. They are pushed out. It is very quiet in the "eye" of the hurricane. Almost no wind blows there.

If a hurricane moves over land,
fierce winds and heavy rain come with
it. There might be a tornado too.
Trees bend or fall.

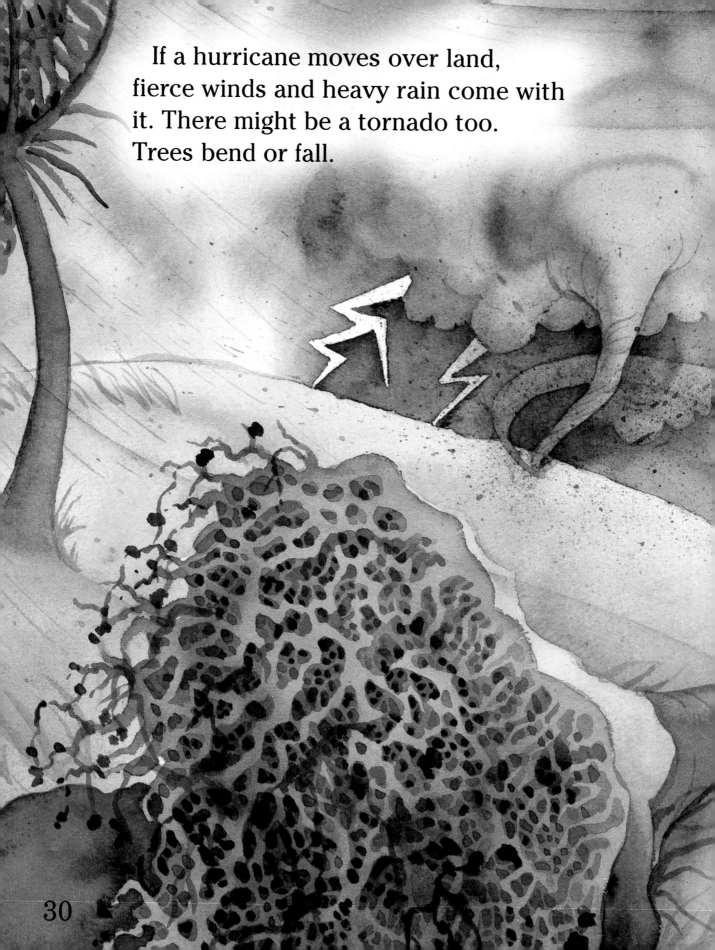

Windows might crack or shatter.
Thunder roars. Lightning flashes.
Floods can cover the land.

Hurricanes can be scary. Today we know when a hurricane will happen. We know when to leave our homes and when to come back. The hurricane might leave a mess, but we will be safe.

Glossary

B

Mom found a **blanket** to help keep me warm.

C

A **cactus** is a desert plant that can live a long time without water.

Cirrus clouds are thin clouds that form high in the sky.

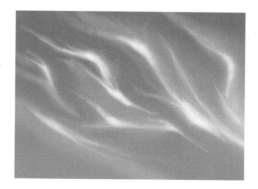

Cumulus clouds are fluffy and form below cirrus clouds.

D

Although there is little rain, lots of plants and animals live in a **desert.**

E

The middle of a hurricane is called the **eye.**

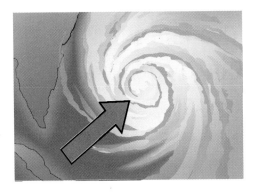

During the **fall,** the temperature gets cooler and some leaves change color and fall to the ground.

The lake was **frozen** after a week of very cold weather.

A **groundhog** digs a burrow to live in.

M

A **mole** spends most of its time in its underground tunnels.

Very few animals live at the top of a high **mountain** because there is no food there.

R

A squirrel is a kind of **rodent.**

The window will **shatter** if a baseball is thrown at it.

Each **snowflake** is different from all the others.

In **summer** the temperature is usually warmer than in the other seasons.

The strong winds were **swirling** loudly today.

T

On a hot summer day the **thermometer** may read 90 degrees Fahrenheit.

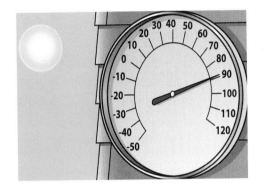

W

Animals gather at a **water hole** to drink some water.

A **wind sock** tells the direction and strength of the wind.

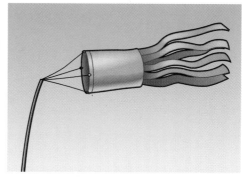

We will fly our kites because it is a **windy** day.

In **winter** the air usually gets colder and in some places it snows.